Mark Pincus and
Zynga

Mark Pincus and
Zynga

SARAH MACHAJEWSKI

ROSEN
PUBLISHING

New York

Published in 2014 by The Rosen Publishing Group, Inc.
29 East 21st Street, New York, NY 10010

Library of Congress Cataloging-in-Publication Data

Machajewski, Sarah.
Mark Pincus and Zynga/Sarah Machajewski.—First edition.
     pages cm.—(Internet biographies)
Includes bibliographical references and index.
ISBN 978-1-4488-9530-4 (library binding)
1. Internet games. 2. Social media—Games. 3. Social networks—
Games. 4. Pincus, Mark. 5. Zynga (Firm) I. Title.
GV1469.15.M345 2014
794.8'1—dc23

                                                    2012040219

Manufactured in the United States of America

CPSIA Compliance Information: Batch #S13YA: For further information, contact Rosen Publishing, New York, New York, at
1-800-237-9932.

Contents

INTRODUCTION

Have you ever logged on to Facebook to water some virtual corn? How about running your own city via your mobile phone? Have you ever played online games with your friends in another state? If you have done any of these things, it's likely that you have Mark Pincus to thank. Pincus, the founder and CEO of Zynga, Inc., has changed the way people play virtual games. Zynga has changed gaming from an isolating and stationary hobby into a way that millions of people interact and communicate with their friends. Zynga's motto, "Connecting the world through games," speaks to its founder's desire to do just that—connect people from around the globe through online social games.

We've become so accustomed to Zynga's games that it's hard to imagine the Internet without them. But before 2005, social gaming was just an abstract idea. For years, dedicated gamers and entrepreneurs thought

Mark Pincus is the founder and current CEO of Zynga, Inc.

about ways to expand gaming beyond a single console. They were excited about connecting millions of people in a way that hadn't been done before. However, it wasn't until Mark Pincus came along that those ideas finally became a reality. With his entrepreneurial spirit and skill for anticipating trends, Pincus saw the potential of gaming in the burgeoning social media movement. By launching Zynga when he did, he was able to, literally and figuratively, get ahead of the game. Through much trial and error, many hardships and successes, and a huge amount of personal and professional dedication, Pincus transformed a small start-up into an Internet juggernaut.

To understand Pincus's and Zynga's role in the growth of social connectivity, one need only look at the founder's life. Known for being bright yet unconventional, Pincus always managed to find opportunities in uncharted places. Whether it was his educational experiences, first jobs out of college, or one of the many start-up companies he founded, his peers have always seen him as a man who defies traditional paths.

His outside-the-box thinking has frequently been met with controversy. Sometimes perceived as ruthless, Pincus has regularly come under fire for doing whatever was needed to help Zynga reach the next level of success. Zynga's growth has been somewhat of a roller coaster ride—a result of Pincus's efforts to adapt to an ever-changing market. Sometimes successful and sometimes not, Pincus's actions as CEO have directly affected the company's reputation and stability in the gaming and social media worlds.

In the time that Zynga has been on the scene, the company has turned the Internet gaming industry on its head. Its trajectory from a small start-up with one poker game to the powerhouse that gave us the enormously popular *FarmVille* and *CityVille* is a testament to Pincus's strengths as an entrepreneur. During his explosive career, he has staked his claim as an industry figurehead with a strong company to match.

CHAPTER 1

From Board Games to Boardrooms

Mark Jonathan Pincus was born on February 13, 1966, in the Lincoln Park neighborhood of Chicago, Illinois. Born to successful parents, he was the only boy in a family of five children. Mark's mother and father held prominent jobs in their community. His mother, Sherri, was an architect. His father, Ted, held many high-profile jobs when Mark was growing up. First he was a public relations adviser to Chicago politicians and then a founding partner at a mergers and acquisitions firm. Mark's parents set the example that hard work was the key to success, and they instilled in their son a desire to achieve great things.

FUN AND GAMES

Mark's parents were very involved in their children's upbringing and fostered a close-knit family environment. They aimed to strike a balance between work and play, especially if they could incorporate life lessons along the way. In particular, they tried to teach their children to think outside the box. One way they did this was by playing games.

Game night at the Pincus household was no ordinary night. At Zynga's five-year anniversary party, Pincus told those in attendance that his "competitive" family regularly played games like charades and Scrabble, but with a twist. Instead of following the games' instructions, the Pincus family made their own rules and changed the games as they played. This fostered an environment of creative thinking. Playing games together with his family allowed the young Mark to look at situations in new and innovative ways, a characteristic that would define his professional career. Above all, the exposure to the social and fun aspects of games planted the seeds of what would become a lifelong interest.

Mark's love of gaming only increased as he got older. In the early 1980s, video games like *Pac-Man* and *Pong* exploded onto the scene in arcades and homes across the country. As a teenager, he became obsessed with trying out any new game that came along. He told the *Chicago Sun-Times*, "My friends and family joked that I wasted my youth playing video games. Who knew it would end up being a career?"

Games have always played a big role in Pincus's life. Here, he is surrounded by some of his favorite games from his childhood, including cards and board games.

Nobody, especially Mark himself, predicted that his early love of games would lead to a successful career as the founder and CEO of Zynga, the largest Internet gaming company in the world. Looking back on his childhood experiences, it may seem evident that gaming was always his destiny. But he wouldn't find that out until much later.

ENTERING THE REAL WORLD

Gaming was a huge part of Mark's childhood, but he also excelled in school. He attended the Francis W. Parker School from kindergarten until the twelfth grade and graduated in 1984. After graduation, he studied economics at the Wharton School of the University of Pennsylvania.

His academic path led him to his first job, as a financial analyst for Lazard Frères. He spent two years at Lazard before leaving to work for Asian Capital Partners in Hong Kong. Later, he went back to school to earn his MBA (master's degree in business administration) from Harvard Business School.

With a bright mind, impressive professional experience, and a prestigious Ivy League educational background, one might assume that Pincus was a natural fit for the corporate world. But, after spending his twenties in various jobs that took him all over the world, he felt unsatisfied with his chosen career path. In an interview with the *Financial Times*, he reflected, "I felt like an expert witness in my twenties—I had a series of jobs where I felt that I had the right answer but was never empowered to make the decision. You were called to the stand, you said what you thought was the right answer, and then you were excused and you find the next day what the decision was. Then you have to live with it and make it successful."

Pincus was frustrated with the lack of leadership and decision-making power that his jobs provided. These feelings only grew with time, and they came to a head as he continued his education.

The Wharton School of the University of Pennsylvania is one of the nation's most prestigious schools. Pincus earned a bachelor's degree in economics from Wharton in 1988.

While at Harvard, Pincus held an internship with Bain & Company as a summer associate. It was a competitive position; as such, most young strivers would have tried to fit in with the office environment in hopes of eventually getting a full-time job offer. Pincus, however, valued the ability to think independently and speak his mind, and his behavior often clashed with the company's expectations.

This conflict came up for Pincus not only at Bain, but also in other jobs and career situations. Many corporate employers expected employees to accept their duties and responsibilities without question. Pincus had a hard time doing this. He would often question the directions given to him. According to an article in *Vanity Fair*, when interviewing for new positions, he would even tell an interviewer when he thought a question was "dumb." Pincus's self-admitted lack of respect for authority would prove to be the catalyst for his venture into entrepreneurship: he was the only intern to graduate business school without a full-time job offer, and he came to the realization that his attitude would deter most big companies from hiring him. With few options and a true resistance to staying in a "normal" job, Pincus started down the path that would eventually lead him to Zynga.

CARVING HIS OWN PATH

Pincus graduated from Harvard Business School in 1993. Two years later, he decided that he'd had enough of the corporate life. He knew that he was smart and that his corporate endeavors had equipped him with the skills he needed to be successful in business. At this point, it was a matter of combining all of his business savvy into one successful idea.

In 1995, Pincus launched his first Internet start-up. He couldn't have picked a better time to do it. The period of the mid-to-late '90s in the United States is often called the Internet boom because of the rapid growth of the Internet and its increasing presence in everyday life. As the Internet grew, the number of Internet-based companies grew alongside it. The rush to create and invest in new Internet companies during that time is known today as the dot-com bubble.

Pincus's start-up, Freeloader, Inc., was one of the first Web-based push technology services. Push technology is a means of getting content to a user who requests it. In today's Internet environment, push technology is very common; for example, it helps us receive e-mails or notifications on an app. In 1995, Pincus was one of the first people to understand that Internet companies needed push technology services. Recognizing an opportunity, he built his company to meet the demand for something people wanted.

Seven months after its launch, Pincus sold Freeloader, Inc., for $38 million. With a full bank account and start-up experience under his belt, he set out to launch another

Pincus and Web designer Elliot Loh collaborate on a project at Tribe.net. This social networking site was one of Pincus's earlier start-ups.

company. In 1997, out of a rented office space, Pincus and two other partners founded Replicase, Inc., also known as Support.com. Support.com provided technology support services to small companies.

As CEO and chairman, Pincus oversaw administrative duties and the company's business plan. Most of all, he was responsible for networking. With the company headquartered in Redwood City, California, and later, Palo Alto, California, Pincus had access to key people in the software and Internet development industry. He knew that he had to make friends in high places in order to be successful. He cultivated good working relationships with investors, programmers, and other important figures. While his focus at the time was growing Support.com, he met influential people and formed relationships that would later help him launch Zynga.

What Is a Start-Up?

A start-up is a new or developing company with an innovative business plan. A start-up can exist in any industry, but most people think of high-tech businesses when they hear the word "start-up."

The entrepreneur behind a start-up must tell investors why his or her company is valuable in order to raise capital to grow the business. Start-ups typically get their funding from angel investors (wealthy individuals who take an interest in the business) and venture capitalists (firms that earn money by investing in new enterprises). Angel investors and venture capitalists sometimes choose to invest their money because they can buy a stake in the company. This gives them some decision-making power and positions them to make money from the company should it become successful.

Raising capital can be very time-consuming for the entrepreneur or founder. In order to secure funding, the entrepreneur needs to have a legitimate business idea and a business plan that is backed up by hard facts and research. He or she has to prove to investors that the idea has the potential to be financially successful.

Start-ups are notoriously high-risk ventures: success isn't guaranteed. Founders dedicate an enormous amount of time, money, and effort into launching a start-up, all of which can be lost if the idea doesn't take off. Start-ups have a high failure rate, but those that do succeed can offer enormous rewards. Google and Facebook are examples of start-ups that have turned their founders into billionaires.

He left Support.com in 2002. With Freeloader, Inc., and Support.com, Pincus's start-up career had concentrated on the data and technology needs of businesses. He aimed to focus his next efforts on something a little more fun—an Internet company with a "social" twist.

GETTING INTO SOCIAL MEDIA

In the early 2000s, more and more people began to use the Internet as a way to keep in touch with other people. E-mail, chat rooms, and instant messaging became popular ways to communicate with others in real time. In addition, a new concept called "social networking" was taking hold. Early social networking consisted of online forums where users could ask and answer questions, upload content, and generally connect with others on the Internet. During this period, Pincus was building a reputation in the Internet entrepreneur community. Located in San Francisco, he wasn't quite in Silicon Valley, but he was close enough to have his foot in the door at companies that would eventually become major influences on social networking. In 2002, he invested in Friendster, one of the first social media sites, and he began to think about creating his own site. He made this idea a reality and formed Tribe Networks, commonly known as Tribe.net, in 2003.

Tribe.net was an online community that allowed users to interact with other users in the same geographic area. Members were able to monitor forums and post content. Tribe.net experienced many ups and downs from 2003 to 2007, facing member backlash, server difficulties, and financial woes. These issues ultimately prevented it from being as successful as some of the other social networking companies. By 2006, Pincus recognized that Tribe.net was failing. He was disappointed that his social network had not succeeded, especially as the industry was growing rapidly.

Tribe.net's failure was humbling, and it taught him many lessons. In an interview with Mediabistro.com, Pincus explained that one of the most important lessons he learned about business was to "fail fast." He said, "I wish I had just failed fast with Tribe. I think that entrepreneurs are always at risk of mistaking stubbornness for conviction and commitment. Just because you'll stick with an idea doesn't necessarily make you a winner, and it could delay you failing and getting to the right answer." Pincus said the experience taught him to test ideas "as cheaply and quickly and often as you can."

Pincus began thinking ahead to his next big idea. He watched the social networking industry grow and change daily. He saw companies trying to come up with the newest and best idea (or, as he told Mediabistro.com, engaging in an "arms race"), and he felt excited about it. He thought about his own interests and how to incorporate them into social networking. His biggest personal interest, stemming from childhood, was gaming. Pincus began thinking and testing. He set his sights on introducing the world to social gaming.

CHAPTER 2

Zynga's Origins

If the mid-to-late '90s saw the birth of the Internet, the early-to-mid '00s saw the growth of a variety of Internet trends. One of the most prominent was the rise of social media. Social media means creating and participating in online communities where people share information, ideas, personal messages, and multimedia content, such as videos. Social media can be accessed by anyone, anywhere, at any time, as long as the person has a computer or other electronic communication device and an Internet connection.

GROWTH OF SOCIAL MEDIA

In the early 2000s, many companies worked furiously to become the next big name in social media. Friendster, Myspace, and Facebook were all in the early development stages as people were becoming interested in online socializing. The Internet made sharing information

Mark Zuckerberg of Facebook (*top*) and Reid Hoffman of LinkedIn (*bottom*) launched their own start-ups that changed the way people use the Internet. Pincus counts them among his friends.

easier than it had ever been. People began spending more time on the Internet, and they began to view it as a forum to share information about themselves. There was a growing interest in the platforms that could help people connect with others.

Social media was on the rise, and key people started to emerge as the founding members and brainpower of this movement. Pincus, still networking and trying to grow Tribe, formed relationships with two important figures: Reid Hoffman, founder of LinkedIn and an executive at PayPal, and Mark Zuckerberg, founder of Facebook. Through these relationships, he learned about where these companies were headed and what their business models were. Being in the company of these innovative entrepreneurs would pay off as he began to think about his next venture.

As time went on, Pincus began reaping the rewards of relationships that he had formed with other Internet entrepreneurs. In 2003, he and Hoffman purchased a groundbreaking social networking patent from SixDegrees.com for $700,000. The patent gave them ownership of a particular method for creating networking databases. This was a huge opportunity for the two entrepreneurs, as all forthcoming social networking sites would have to pay them royalties if they chose to use the same method.

In addition, purchasing the SixDegrees patent created other openings for Pincus, including getting his foot in the door at Facebook before it became exponentially successful. The purchase helped spur a relationship between the two Marks (Pincus and Zuckerberg), which would eventually lead to an important relationship between their companies. Pincus became an early investor at Facebook, and as of this writing, he still owns 0.5 percent of the company. He also connected with other young companies and became an angel investor for future hits, such as Napster and Xoom. But his list of angel investments did not include any gaming companies. He was saving that industry for himself.

WHY GAMING?

Pincus was in the right place at the right time to capitalize on the social networking trend. However, in order to achieve the level of success he desired, he needed to differentiate himself. His social networking experience at Tribe.net, in addition to his friendships with other entrepreneurs, allowed him to see what users wanted, where the social media trend was heading, and what types of things could be successful. When it became clear that Tribe.net would not succeed, Pincus decided he wanted to focus on something that could work inside of an already existing social media platform. He found his answer in apps.

Apps are software features that can be installed on and used via a social network. During this period, many

A teen uses a laptop to log in to her Facebook account. On Facebook, she can see what her friends are sharing in the social media sphere, including the games they play.

developers focused on apps that could be shared virally, such as photos, virtual gifts, and "pokes" on Facebook. However, Pincus believed there was a market for apps that were more interactive and fun. He thought about his own interests, especially something that he had loved his whole life: games.

He saw tremendous opportunity in social gaming apps. This area would allow him to combine two of his interests—social media and games—without having to launch his own social network. By developing apps for a pre-existing company like Facebook or Myspace, Pincus realized that he could bring his product to people who were

Naming the Company

In its early days, Zynga started off under the name PresidioMedia. It was a fine name, but it was generic. Pincus wanted to make his company stand out. He knew a catchy name would make it memorable to users. He also knew it would help grow his brand image. The American Marketing Association (AMA) defines "brand" as a "name, term, design, symbol, or any other feature that identifies one seller's good or service as distinct from those of other sellers." To Pincus, or any other entrepreneur, a catchy name was key to making his social gaming company a success.

Pincus wanted Zynga to have the resonance of brands like Coca-Cola or Nike—companies whose names make them immediately recognizable. He started brainstorming and sought the advice of an adviser and friend, Fred Wilson. Wilson was a

Pincus's dog, Zinga, inspired the name of his gaming company.

venture capitalist with experience launching technology companies, so Pincus valued his opinion. He called Wilson and listed some ideas that he liked. Then he mentioned a name that held a lot of meaning: Zinga, the name of his pet bulldog. This name caught Wilson's ear as catchy and original, and he advised Pincus to choose it as the brand name. However, there was only one problem—the domain name Zinga.com was unavailable! Pincus had tried to buy the domain name for eight years, to no avail.

After pitching more ideas to Wilson, other friends, and colleagues at PresidioMedia, Pincus finally found a way around the problem. He simply changed the "i" to "y," and Zynga was born.

Since then, dogs have played a major role in the day-to-day operations at Zynga. The company's logo features the silhouette of an American bulldog next to the name. Employees are allowed to bring their dogs to work, and they have grassy areas where the dogs play during the day. Zynga's headquarters are even known as "The Dog House." Sadly, Zinga the bulldog passed away shortly after Zynga was founded. Pincus loved his dog very much, and naming the company after her has been a great way to honor her memory.

already connecting with others online. Games could simply be another way for them to interact with their friends.

Pincus told Mediabistro.com, "What I thought was the ultimate thing you can do—once you bring all of your friends and their friends together—is play games. And I've always been a closet gamer, but I never have the time and can never get all of my friends together in one place. So the power of my friends already being there and connected, and then adding games, seemed like a big idea."

To him, gaming and social networks seemed like a natural pair. However, up until this point, most video games were only single player, or they required everyone to gather in one place to play together. The key was to create an app that could be installed on a social network and shared by any number of people.

Pincus's next logical step was to build a company to answer this need. He needed money to finance his newest start-up, developers to help him create the gaming technology, and most of all, a social network (or two) on which he could debut his games.

ZYNGA'S EARLY DAYS

Mark Pincus's involvement at Tribe.net came to an end in 2006. He spent a few months considering his next move. Then, in April 2007, he formed his fourth start-up,

PresidioMedia. In the company's first months, Pincus focused on gathering the best minds in the business. He looked for employees with a good work ethic and dedication to his company's mission. He assembled a small team of eight people: Eric Schiermeyer, Michael Luxton, Justin Waldron, Kyle Stewart, Scott Dale, Steve Schoettler, Kevin Hagan, and Andrew Trader.

In 2007, big things were happening in the social media world. User counts were up across the board, and social networks like Myspace and Facebook were competing against each other to become the biggest and the best. Pincus had held onto the idea of social gaming for a long time; now was his chance to make a move.

The team at PresidioMedia began developing video games. They had some criteria to follow. For one, the games had to be operable inside of a social networking Web site. They solved this problem by making browser-based games. The team also had to think carefully about the nature of the games: they had to be multiplayer, fun, and engaging. Finally, they had to be easy to use.

In these early testing phases, Pincus thought back to the lessons he had learned in his corporate jobs and earlier start-ups. He gave his team the freedom to experiment and test many different types of games. And they found ways to complete the development process cheaply and quickly.

PresidioMedia debuted its first games on Myspace. Other gaming companies were having some success on this social network with ad-based games. Ad-based games make money by showing advertisements. When a player clicks on an ad, the advertiser pays the gaming company money. PresidioMedia made most of its early money this way. Myspace was a great launching point for its games, but Pincus had a gut feeling that the future of his company would lie elsewhere.

In May 2007, Facebook opened up an applications programming interface to outside companies. Pincus was

Zynga's logo features the silhouette of an American bulldog in honor of Pincus's beloved dog.

excited—the time had finally come to get his games on the Internet's hottest social network. However, Pincus had a little detail to take care of first: the company's name. In July 2007, he changed the name of his company to Zynga, Inc., and it has kept this name ever since.

Zynga's team worked to craft the perfect Facebook game. After much trial and error, the company launched *Texas Hold 'Em Poker*. The choice to do a virtual card game made sense. Consumer interest in poker had been on the rise since 2003. Zynga was simply taking it to the next level by making it a virtual experience. It would just be a matter of time before Zynga learned if its first major move was a success or failure.

CHAPTER 3

Getting in the Game

Texas Hold 'Em Poker debuted on Facebook in September 2007. It was the first virtual poker game to debut on a social network. The game had many qualities that attracted users. For one, it was free. It was accessible—anybody with a Facebook account could log in and play. It was also simple. Most important, it created a new way for people to connect with their friends.

A STRONG HAND

People around the country frequently held poker nights with their friends. However, there was a catch: everybody needed to be in the same place at the same time. With *Texas Hold 'Em Poker,* friends could have poker nights even if they were on other sides of the world. And many people did just that.

Pincus had always believed that games were a natural way to connect with friends and that games had business potential online. The large number of Facebook users who started playing *Texas Hold 'Em Poker* was all the proof that Pincus needed that he was truly on to something.

Another component to the poker game's success was that users didn't have to play against their friends. *Texas Hold 'Em Poker* allowed users to play against anyone, as long as they were logged in to Facebook. Users embraced this idea wholeheartedly. Playing *Texas Hold 'Em Poker* against people they didn't know greatly expanded their social networks. Now, users had the opportunity to become friends with people they might never have met in real life. The uniting factor was a social game.

Zynga employees work hard on *Zynga Poker*—which originally launched as *Texas Hold 'Em Poker*—at the company's San Francisco headquarters in 2011.

Pincus told Mediabistro.com, "I've always said that social networks are like a great cocktail party: You're happy at first to see your good friends, but the value of the cocktail party is in the weak ties. It's the people you wouldn't have thought of meeting; it's the friends-of-friends." Even before Zynga took off, Pincus had known that games had the power to bring people together. This game proved that.

Today, *Texas Hold 'Em Poker* is known as *Zynga Poker*. According to Zynga.com, it has more than thirty-five million active users, and it is the fourth-most-popular game on Facebook. The company regularly updates its blog with gaming tips, strategies, and incentives for players.

A MAN WITH A PLAN

With one success under his belt, Mark Pincus showed disbelievers that social gaming could work. *Texas Hold 'Em Poker* was the first successful game, but it certainly wouldn't be the last. Pincus knew this. He thought it was time for him to take Zynga to the next level. This would involve developing, testing, and launching new games.

In order to make his dream a reality, he needed money. Zynga was experiencing success, but the company needed more money to cover operating costs and pay for essentials like employee salaries and new game development.

Pincus knew that raising capital would be a lengthy process, but he was determined to succeed. He already had relationships with powerful investors, but he was missing one very important thing: a business plan. Zynga was profitable because of *Texas Hold 'Em Poker*, but Pincus needed to show investors that Zynga was special. A good business plan would demonstrate how Zynga would make money and be successful in the long term. If Pincus could develop this kind of plan, he knew that raising money would be a breeze.

In order to raise capital, Pincus developed a business plan he could share with investors. In an article on VentureBeat.com, Dean Takahashi explained that the core of Zynga's business was "metric-driven, combining intuition and data...[Zynga] learned what users wanted and modified its games quickly, sometimes overnight, to better provide what the users wanted." At the time, other gaming companies did not operate in this way. This business model provided a clear picture of how the company would be successful. Although it would change slightly as the years went on, this early model set the company apart.

RAISING CAPITAL

It wasn't difficult to find investors that were interested in Zynga. For one, the company was profitable. Second, player counts were growing daily and it looked as if this would continue. These factors won over investors and

Fred Wilson, one of Pincus's mentors and friends, played a huge role in securing capital for Zynga.

gave them faith that Zynga would be a smart investment. Fred Wilson, whose firm Union Square Ventures invested in Zynga, explained to the *New York Times*, "People already love to play casual games...but when you take a casual game and stick it inside a social network, it becomes way more exciting. This is like pouring gasoline on fire."

This factor alone made investors willing to contribute to Zynga. On January 15, 2008, the company announced that it had raised its first round of capital. It secured $10 million in investments from venture capital firms, including Union Square Ventures, Foundry Group, and Avalon Ventures. Some of Pincus's personal friends, like Reid Hoffman and Peter Thiel, invested, too.

With the new capital, Zynga's team focused on game development. They quickly scrapped games that weren't working and tested every idea in the book. As the company developed new games, it kept a close eye on Facebook. Facebook was constantly changing its platform. This kept developers on their toes because they had to modify their work quickly and often. Luckily, with Pincus as CEO, the Zynga team was used to these kinds of demands.

Only a few short months after the first round of investments, Pincus worked to secure more. In a July 2008 press release, Zynga announced that the company

Mentor Bing Gordon

Mark Pincus's mentor, Bing Gordon, was an experienced executive in the video game industry. Over the course of his career, he became a key figure in the field of venture capital. Today, he serves on the board of directors for a number of Internet companies.

Gordon's path to success started in 1968, when he entered Yale University as an undergraduate. He studied drama and literature. After graduation, he stayed on the East Coast for a few years, working odd jobs and trying to figure out what career he wanted to pursue. He liked the performing arts, but he wanted to pursue graduate-level studies in business. He entered Stanford University's MBA program in 1978. Upon graduation, he worked in a series of high-profile advertising jobs, eventually ending up at the video gaming company Electronic Arts (EA) in 1982.

Bing Gordon, partner at venture capital firm Kleiner Perkins, has served as an adviser and friend to Pincus since they met in 2008.

Electronic Arts was one of the first video game companies in the industry. In its thirty-year history, it has been a pioneer of computer games for the home, publishing many groundbreaking games that changed the video game industry. EA has published extremely popular video game titles like *The Sims* and *Madden NFL*, as well as other notable franchises under companies that it has acquired. This includes PopCap Games, creator of the popular Internet games *Bejeweled* and *Plants vs. Zombies.*

Gordon served as EA's chief creative officer for ten years. He held a variety of other roles until 2008, when he announced that he was leaving to become a partner at venture capital firm Kleiner Perkins. A month after joining the firm, Kleiner Perkins invested a hefty sum in Zynga. Gordon became an important figure in Pincus's life. Gordon's mentor role has made the two men close, and he has always stood by Pincus through the ups and downs of Zynga's operations. In 2010, he told VentureBeat.com, "I have high regard for Mark Pincus as a visionary. He combined the best of the Web, games, and social. It never occurred to anyone those would come together."

had raised an astonishing $29 million in investment capital. No other gaming company had raised that amount of money at once, especially not one that had been operating for only a year. The investment firm Kleiner Perkins contributed most of the funds.

Just as importantly, the firm introduced Mark Pincus to Bing Gordon. Gordon was partner at Kleiner Perkins and a former employee at the gaming company Electronic Arts. This proved to be a fateful meeting. In 2008, Gordon became a member of Zynga's board of directors. He also became Pincus's mentor, guiding him through his tenure as CEO. Pincus and Bing's relationship benefited Zynga's reputation and helped continue the company's rise to success.

Of the many things that Gordon did for Pincus, one of the most important was introducing him to a man named Mark Skaggs. Gordon knew Skaggs as a top developer at Electronic Arts, and he brought him over to Zynga's team in late 2008. Skaggs would later go on to develop Zynga's explosively popular *FarmVille* game.

FRIENDS ON ALL SOCIAL NETWORKS

Pincus was dedicated to making Zynga the biggest Internet gaming company in the industry. In its first year, the team at Zynga developed games for multiple platforms. The two biggest at the time were Facebook and Myspace, but there was no way to know for sure which company would be more successful in the long run. Pincus did not want to choose between the two; he believed that having an exclusive relationship with one company would cause Zynga to miss out on players from other networks. Zynga developed games for all platforms while the social networks battled it out for the number-one spot.

Through working on various start-ups as well as his angel investments, Pincus had cultivated a good relationship with Facebook's founder, Mark Zuckerberg. This let him see Facebook's plans for future growth. This was important because Zynga's browser-based games depended on Facebook's activity. Pincus observed Facebook's actions and tweaked Zynga's products accordingly.

Facebook's popularity took off in 2007 and 2008. Zynga was with it every step of the way. At the same time, Myspace started to lose users. After about a year, it was clear that Facebook had won the social networking competition. However, Zynga continued to develop games for both. Pincus decided to keep all of his options open, but he focused Zynga's efforts mostly on Facebook. The two companies have been intertwined ever since.

Over the years, Pincus has maintained relationships with many social platforms despite Zynga's loyalty to Facebook. Today, Zynga offers games on Facebook,

Myspace, the iPhone and iPad, Android devices, Yahoo!, and FarmVille.com.

GENERATING REVENUE

As CEO of a young company in a new industry, Pincus had to figure out how to turn Zynga into a revenue-generating company. One problem that stood in the way of making money was the fact that Zynga's games were free to play. As with other online games, players did not have to spend money to access the games—in most cases, all they needed was a social media account, and this did not make money for the company.

Pincus knew that he needed to find a way around this. He had to show his investors that the

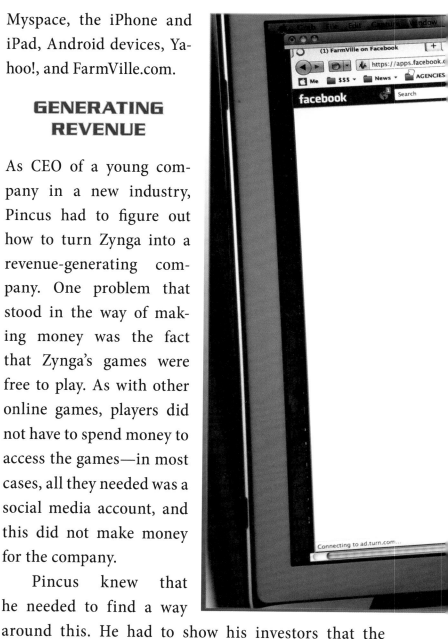

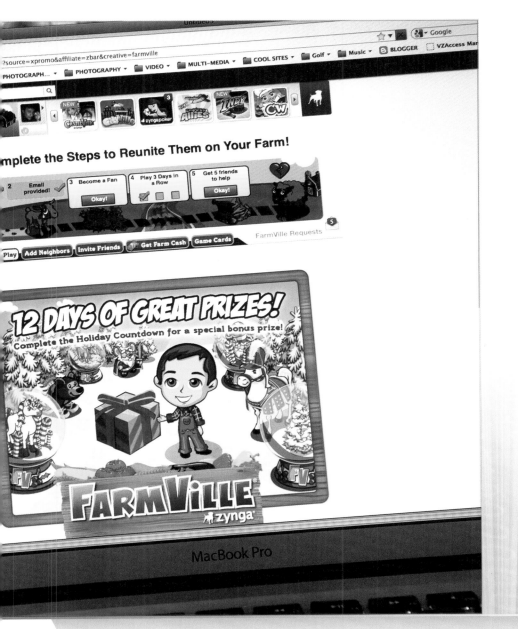

FarmVille players had the chance to play for holiday bonus prizes in December 2011, as shown in this screenshot. Zynga offers prizes within its games as part of a revenue-generating strategy.

company was profitable. He directed the Zynga team to explore any avenue that had the potential to make money. Some of the ideas that they tried early on did generate revenue, but they had a negative effect on the game and the player experience.

One way that Zynga tried to increase profits was to include software tools created by third-party companies inside their games. In these business partnerships, both outside companies and Zynga had the opportunity to make money from the relationship. Third-party companies wanted to work with Zynga because they could promote and distribute their products to the games' players. For example, in *Texas Hold 'Em Poker*, Zynga offered poker chips to players if they downloaded a toolbar from an outside company. The company paid Zynga for every player that downloaded the tool. Once the toolbar was on a user's computer, it was difficult to remove. Today, such software is known as malware, or malicious software. Types of malware include adware, which automatically shows pop-up ads or other advertising, and spyware, which collects and transmits data on the user.

Zynga did not employ these methods forever, but the company regularly changed the features and ads inside of its games, looking for the quickest and easiest way to make money. While this business model made sense for Zynga's profitability, it compromised the players' experience.

Further, these strategies created a public relations problem for Pincus after he acknowledged them at the 2009 Startup@Berkeley conference. He gave a lecture at the conference about launching a successful start-up. He offered tips, strategies, and insight into how he took Zynga from a start-up to an Internet juggernaut. Attendees listened intently as Pincus said something that would come back to haunt him: "I did every horrible thing in the book just to get revenues right away... We did anything possible to just get revenues so that we could grow and be a real business." People were shocked. They couldn't believe that the CEO of Zynga admitted that his company did whatever it needed to do to make money.

Attendees clapped nervously while bloggers passed on Pincus's message to the Internet. His reputation took a significant hit. Overnight, his image changed from a widely admired CEO to a greedy capitalist that tried to take advantage of people. Three months later, Pincus told *Details* magazine that he "didn't mean to be so crass."

He acknowledged his mistake, but he has since been known as a controversial figure. This was only one of a number of controversies that Pincus would face.

CHAPTER 4

Zynga Takes Off

In mid-2008, Zynga's player numbers were increasing daily, and the company was becoming more profitable. With almost $40 million in capital raised, Zynga had developed clout in the social gaming world. It had plenty of capital in the bank to expand its business and launch new games.

But the company was still relatively new. The team was still learning what users wanted from social games and what could be successful. Mark Pincus's next goal was to recreate *Texas Hold 'Em Poker*'s success, but on an even bigger level. He needed his team to do whatever it could to make that happen.

Pincus directed his team to test as many ideas as possible. The development team constantly tested and retested games, trying to find the formula for the perfect social game. Pincus stopped development on games that didn't appear to be successful and fired employees who weren't working hard enough. He also started examining what outside developers were doing to try to find interesting content for Zynga.

YOVILLE AND MAFIA WARS

In 2008, Zynga acquired, or bought, a game called *YoVille* from an independent game developer. User counts for the game rose to 150,000, something that had not been achieved under the other company. This set a significant precedent: Zynga, with its hefty bank account, was able to take out the competition by acquiring a game from an outside developer and making it more successful. This business strategy was something Zynga would repeat. This strategy would become a source of controversy; while acquisitions help Zynga, some people feel that it prevents other, smaller companies from becoming successful.

Another controversy cropped up in 2008 when Zynga debuted *Mafia Wars*. *Mafia Wars* allowed users to control their own mafia. The game logged millions of users and solidified Zynga's status as social media's strongest gaming company. However, PsychoMonkey LLC, developer of a game called *Mob Wars*, believed that Zynga had copied its game. The games looked similar and had the same purpose. Upset over the similarities, the company filed a lawsuit against Zynga. Zynga settled out of court.

Despite the controversy, *YoVille* and *Mafia Wars* were the first examples of what most people have come to

Zynga's San Francisco headquarters runs like a well-oiled machine during game launches. Here, employees prepare for the launch of *Mafia Wars 2*.

now identify as a typical Zynga game. They were simple one-player games that let users control their own virtual world. Launching single-player games might seem antithetical to the "social" aspect of social gaming, but that's where Facebook became important. Updates from the games appeared in the players' social media accounts, showing their progress to their network of friends. This proved to be a make-or-break feature of the new games' success.

Initially, some analysts criticized Zynga's browser-based games for being totally dependent on Facebook and other social networks. In a talk at the University of California, Berkeley, Pincus himself admitted that Zynga "lived and died" by the changes Facebook made to its software platforms. But there was no denying that Facebook had a unique power to make something go viral. Seeing many Facebook friends with activity on a Zynga game was a virtual version of making something popular by word of mouth. For this reason, Pincus didn't mind that Zynga was in Facebook's pocket.

FARMVILLE

Mark Skaggs told the story of *FarmVille* at the 2011 Game Developers Conference. According to Skaggs, the idea for *FarmVille* came from Bing Gordon. He said Gordon called him into his office on one fateful day in 2009. He put his feet up on the desk and said, "Why don't you make a farm game?" Pincus agreed this was a good idea and approved the development of what would become one of Zynga's biggest games ever.

Meanwhile, a small company called SlashKey had launched a game called *FarmTown*. It was similar to

Mark Skaggs is the senior vice president of product development at Zynga. He oversaw the development and launch of popular games such as *FarmVille* and *CityVille*.

early farm games for video gaming consoles. It allowed users to control their own virtual farms, including raising livestock and growing crops. Pincus observed the newly debuted farm game and knew that Zynga could do better. He also knew that he had only a short time before interest in the farm concept petered out. He assembled a team of developers, led by Skaggs, and demanded a quick turnaround on the game. The developers' time restraints were so tight that they had to borrow avatars from *YoVille* instead of creating new characters. The team also planned to include at least twelve props in the game, but the short schedule forced them to launch with only nine. *FarmVille* launched on Facebook on June 19, 2009.

FarmVille's launch was quiet but successful. The *Wall Street Journal* reported that it had one hundred thousand users on its first day. Within two months, user counts had reached eleven million. From there, it took only a few short months for the game to go viral. By December 2009, *FarmVille* was up to seventy million active users a day. The numbers kept growing, and Zynga's team, especially Pincus, sat in awe of the fact that they had created the most popular social game ever. According to Zynga's blog, the game was the number-one Facebook game from April 2009 to December 2010. If people hadn't heard of Zynga by this time, the *FarmVille* phenomenon certainly changed that.

There were several reasons why *FarmVille* had such a hold on people. For one, it was easy to use. Users simply logged in to Facebook and accessed the game. With a few clicks of a mouse, they could water virtual corn, tend to virtual cows, and sell the produce and goods they produced on their farm. Second, it was the quintessence of a social game. Users were able to visit their friends' farms and become their neighbors. They could send gifts and watch their friends' progress while managing their own game. *FarmVille*'s popularity meant one thing to Pincus: his predictions about social gaming were right. *FarmVille* brought millions of people together through one unifying factor: a game.

SELLING VIRTUAL GOODS

FarmVille was a cash cow for Zynga. Although the game was free to play, Zynga made money by offering virtual goods, a concept it had introduced in previous games. Virtual goods are add-ons that users can purchase for their games. They help improve the player's experience by making the game better or faster. In the case of *Farm-Ville*, people cared so much about their farms that they were willing to pay for virtual goods. People could also send gifts to their friends' farms as long as they paid for them. One of *FarmVille*'s most successful virtual goods was a "withering tool," which helped rescue failing crops. This encouraged people to keep playing, and it kept users

FarmVille was so popular that it prompted the launch of a sequel, *FarmVille 2*. As shown in this image, players can tend to a pumpkin patch and interact with their friends.

online for longer periods of time.

Zynga reaped huge profits from the sale of virtual goods. Pincus explained to MIT's *Technology Review* that people spend money on virtual goods because they care about their games. He said that virtual goods enhance the gaming experience by making gameplay easier and more successful. People's available playing time is limited, he explained, so if they can pay to get to the next level faster, they will. This analysis of a player's motivation speaks to Pincus's keen sense of what players want and need, something that has helped him launch game after game successfully.

Pincus had no problem taking full credit for the

virtual goods concept. He told *Details* magazine in 2010, "We were the first ones to figure out virtual goods and social pay, and we've helped the whole industry."

The demographic that played *FarmVille* also contributed to the game's success. The average *FarmVille* user was female and between the ages of twenty-five and forty-five. Zynga had opened a world of completely new gamers; they weren't college students, but rather, middle-aged female adults. Some speculated that *FarmVille* was popular because these players used fifteen- to twenty-minute gaming sessions as a way to relax after work or take a break from child rearing and other adult responsibilities. The demographic also made Zynga extremely profitable be-

cause unlike typical college students, these older players had money to spend on virtual goods.

Kyra Wilson of Vermont tends to her virtual farm from her home computer. Wilson is an example of the new demographic that *FarmVille* reached.

Zynga brought in millions of users and millions of dollars, thanks to the sale of virtual goods. In a 2009 interview, Pincus told Charlie Rose that virtual goods "made Zynga profitable for eight straight quarters."

With Zynga's growth came a whole host of other factors to consider, such as the company's corporate philosophy and the way that it managed its employees. Until this point, the company had been tackling these questions on a day-to-day basis. Now the CEO of one of the world's most successful Internet companies, Pincus had to sit down and carefully think about his management style and Zynga's operating principles.

"ARE YOU CEO OF SOMETHING?"

Mark Pincus used the lessons that he had learned from his past professional experiences to help cultivate Zynga's success. Part of his approach was demanding the best from his employees. In the past, Pincus had felt stifled by his lack of power and control over his responsibilities. He was determined to keep this from happening to Zynga's employees, and so, as he told the *Financial Times*, he challenged each person to "be a CEO of something."

In Pincus's view, to be a CEO of something means you have to choose a project and completely own it. You must take an idea and see it through to fruition. He had first tested this management style at Support.com, his second start-up. In 2010 Pincus told the *New York Times*, "One thing I did at my second company was to put white sticky sheets on the wall, and I put everyone's name on one of the sheets, and I said, 'By the end of the week, everybody needs to write what you're CEO of, and it needs to be something really meaningful.' And that way, everyone knows who's CEO of what…And it was really effective. People liked it. And there was nowhere to hide."

Pincus adopted this method at Zynga, knowing that his employees would produce good work if they felt important. It also helped ensure that tasks would get done. By having employees take ownership of responsibilities, they could be held accountable to do their jobs.

Pincus respected his employees' contributions and aimed to demonstrate that through his leadership style. In an interview with the *New York Times*, he remarked that "being a true meritocracy" is something he really values. He said, "The only way people will have the trust to give their all to their job is if they feel like their contribution is recognized and valued."

GAME DEVELOPMENT UNDER PINCUS

While Mark Pincus is sometimes viewed as a controversial figure in the gaming industry, most people cannot deny that he has a special touch when it comes to social games. Having been a gamer all his life, he seemed to have a unique perspective on what would make a game successful.

The Zynga team works diligently on one of the company's virtual games from a satellite office in Austin, Texas.

The Zynga team became experts at churning out successful games. Once their formula was perfected, it was just a matter of replicating it. After *FarmVille*, the developers focused on creating different kinds of virtual worlds. Zynga launched software that involved Wild West towns, cities, and pet stores, among others. The company continued to sell virtual goods and turn a nice profit. Essentially, Pincus had figured out the secret to making money on products that were only real inside of a computer screen. Jeffrey Katzenberg, Dreamworks CEO and Zynga board member, told *Vanity Fair*, "What Mark has figured out is just amazing."

At the 2010 D.I.C.E. Summit, Zynga developers shared some of their secrets. According to an article on VentureBeat .com, developers said they spend about $100,000 to $300,000 developing games over the course of four to five weeks. They said they test new features with 5 percent of the gaming audience and scrap things that aren't working before investing too much time or money in them. Finally, they revealed that they pay attention to "the reach of a game, its retention rate, and revenue generated." All of these factors help the Zynga team develop games in the most efficient way possible.

Pincus was also pursuing a marketing opportunity—cross-promotion of games and other services. It made sense in theory, but the way it actually played out brought on a storm of controversy that followed Pincus and Zynga throughout 2010.

CHAPTER 5

Weathering the Storm

Zynga was the first social gaming company to sell virtual goods within its applications. People were interested in how much money Zynga was actually bringing in, and how: Was it mainly through virtual goods? Was it through advertising? Zynga was a private company at the time, so it did not have to release these details about its earnings.

Business analysts kept a close eye on the social gaming movement as it grew in popularity. They kept track of what the games offered and the advertising and commercial offers that accompanied them. People were used to seeing advertisements in games. Every company did it, and it was accepted as part of the reason why games were "free." Commercial offers were another matter, and they created a problem for Zynga.

COMMERCIAL OFFERS

Some of Zynga's users will-ingly paid money for virtual goods and in-game currency, but it was a small percentage. For those who did not want to pay for these items, Zynga hawked commercial offers. Commercial offers are goods or services that a player can sign up for in exchange for in-game currency. On the surface, the player seems to be getting in-game currency for free. In reality, the offers require a credit card number and e-mail address to sign up. Later, the player may get hit with spam e-mails or un-expected credit card charges for a subscription that he or she didn't want. Many people consider this practice

unethical because users get the impression they are get-ting something for free when they really aren't. They end

Pincus has come under fire for some of his business practices. He worked hard to repair his image after several public relations gaffes.

up handing over sensitive personal and financial infor-mation even though they do not fully understand the fine print of the offer. It is widely perceived as a scam, since it is done in the sole interests of the businesses that benefit from it.

Zynga had commercial offer deals with many compa-nies such as Netflix and Offerplay. For every player that sub-scribed to these businesses' services through a Zynga game, Zynga received a cut of the profits. Zynga had millions of players, so it had the potential to make a great deal of money from these deals. Indeed, Andrew Trader, a top executive at Zynga, told the *San Francisco Chronicle* in 2009 that half of Zynga's revenues came from the sale of virtual goods. The other half, he said, came from commercial offers. This meant that Zynga was potentially making millions of dollars by misleading or confusing users. People were upset, and blog-gers and analysts took notice.

The situation came to a head in late 2009, when TechCrunch.com published an article titled "Scamville." In the article, author Michael Arrington commented on the un-ethical nature of Zynga's commercial offers. To Arrington, it wasn't that Zynga was making money—it was that it was done in a questionable way. The fallout from this article was significant. Zynga lost a fair number of users. Players started to feel hesitant about playing. But most of all, it posed a se-vere threat to the future of Zynga's business model. On one hand, it seemed nearly impossible to continue including commercial offers in the game now that so many people were aware of—and offended by—the strategy. On the other hand, the company made a huge amount of money from commercial offers and couldn't fathom removing them. Pincus had a problem on his hands, one that would not be easy to solve.

To make matters worse, once Facebook learned of these allegations, it temporarily shut down Zynga's games as a sign of good faith to its users. This was the tipping point. Zynga had no choice but to remove the commercial offers from its games. In November 2009, Pincus posted a public response to the issue on his blog. He wrote:

[Arrington] raises good points about "scammy" advertisers and the bad user experience they create. I agree with him and others that some of these offers misrepresent and hurt our industry...we need to be more aggressive and have revised our service level agreements with these providers requiring them to filter and police offers prior to posting on their networks. We have also removed all mobile ads until we see any that offer clear user value.

People in the industry, including the staff at TechCrunch.com, applauded Pincus for admitting his mistake. He recognized the problem, confronted it publicly, and took steps to change Zynga's practices. This bolstered

Copycats and Lawsuits

Zynga is the number-one social gaming company in the industry. Although other gaming companies emerged around the same time, they have not matched Zynga's popularity or player counts. One of Zynga's biggest competitors is a company called Playdom. Like Zynga, Playdom produces browser-based games for social networks. Because of their similarities, the companies have produced similar games. They have also attracted employees with similar skills. At one point, tensions between the companies escalated to the point that Zynga took legal action against Playdom.

In 2009, four of Zynga's employees left the company to work for Playdom. Instead of making a clean break, they took with them some of Zynga's most private information about game development and future plans. The documents outlined how Zynga made its games successful—something that was invaluable to their new employer.

When Zynga caught wind of this, it filed a lawsuit against Playdom, accusing it of stealing trade secrets. In the discovery process of the court proceedings, Zynga's lawyers uncovered e-mails between Playdom executives that explicitly stated that they hated Mark Pincus. Zynga used this information to try to prove that Playdom took its employees and secrets purposely—something that the judge weighed heavily. The court ordered that Playdom could not use Zynga's secrets.

his reputation as well as Zynga's. This was another instance in which a public gaffe became a learning moment for Pincus. He learned how to handle a public relations crisis with grace.

GRAPPLING WITH FACEBOOK'S DEMANDS

In spring of 2010, Pincus faced yet another issue. This time it involved Facebook. In an effort to streamline all of its apps, Facebook demanded that third-party developers start using Facebook credits as in-game currency. Further, as TechCrunch.com reported, Facebook demanded that it receive a 30 percent cut of all currency profits. Zynga had been paying only 10 percent up until this point. Pincus was outraged.

Relations between the two companies grew strained. Pincus did not want to hand over more money to Facebook. Instead of acquiescing to the company's demands, he threatened to break away completely. Pincus began to prep his company to launch its own platform, FarmVille.com.

Facebook continued to put pressure on Zynga, but Pincus did not back down. He began to prep his team for their departure. This was risky, since Zynga's browser-based games had until then depended on Facebook. Zynga's success had started on Facebook, and the social network was critical to the social and viral aspects of the games.

Over at Facebook, executives were starting to get nervous. Zynga was extremely important to them. The potential loss in revenue and users caused by Zynga's departure was significant. Both companies had achieved success because of their working relationship. Zynga grew because Facebook provided a social aspect to the games; Facebook grew, in part, because so many users logged in to play games. The breakup would have been damaging to both companies. The Internet world waited with bated breath as tensions mounted.

Zynga has a reputation for being a casual and fun place to work. Employees are even allowed to bring their dogs to the workplace.

Facebook took Pincus's threats seriously. In a few weeks, the two Marks came to an agreement. On May 18, 2010, Facebook and Zynga announced that the companies had entered into a five-year partnership. In a joint press release, they stated that the agreement "increases their shared commitment to social gaming on Facebook and expands use of Facebook Credits in Zynga's games." The partnership preserved the relationship between the two Internet giants, and it saved Zynga from having to start over on its own platform.

At the *Wall Street Journal's* 2012 All Things Digital conference, Pincus said that Facebook "is really important to us...they provide this social graph and identity so that our games can be instantly social without any work on [the user's] part...that's kind of an amazing, magical thing that they provide." Pincus has long recognized that Facebook is a key component to Zynga's success. The partnership was a savvy way to overcome their differences. With the Facebook dispute out of the way, Pincus faced a new controversy, but this time it was under his own roof.

EMPLOYEE LIFE AT ZYNGA

Zynga started in 2007 with a small group of developers. The original team consisted of only eight people, some of whom were friends with Pincus or had worked with him at his other companies. Today, the company Web site states that Zynga has almost three thousand full-time employees. The staff has been through ups and downs with the company. In recent years, differing reports about Zynga's corporate culture have hit the news—some positive, and some negative.

Pincus set out to create a fun and playful environment at Zynga. It seemed only natural to create a fun environment for employees who were creating games. Part of making Zynga an enjoyable place to work was making it a casual environment. Employees at Zynga are allowed to wear jeans and bring their dogs to work. They enjoy perks like free lunches and dry cleaning, all paid for by the company. Zynga's San Francisco headquarters, known as "The Dog House," even has games and other fun items in the lobby area. Pincus created this corporate culture because he wanted his employees to want to come to work. He told the *Financial Times*, "I like to say that with Zynga, we're trying to build a house we want to live in. I'm trying to make something that feels more unique and homely to people."

However, employee life at Zynga hasn't been all fun and games. According to an article in the *New York Times*, in fall 2011 many of Zynga's employees used the quarterly staff survey to voice dissatisfaction with Pincus's leadership style. Some sent dozens of e-mails complaining about long hours and stressful deadlines. They said that Zynga was a high-pressure environment where employees faced demotion or termination if they—or their games—

Zynga employees spend all day working on games, but in their free time they get to play them, too! The Zynga headquarters provides several fun outlets for employees in their downtime.

underperformed. Further, each game had its own team that worked independently of all the other teams; this bred a fiercely competitive environment.

Pincus did not take the results of the survey lightly. A few days later, he called a companywide meeting and read selected comments out loud. He said that he took the employees' concerns to heart and was committed to fixing the problems to make Zynga a better company.

In the following months, Pincus made an effort to change Zynga's working conditions as well as his own managerial style. The *New York Times* noted that Zynga rolled out focus groups for employees and expanded teams. Employees would get the week off before a game's launch and experience more reasonable deadlines. As for Pincus, he dedicated many hours to working with Zynga's "chief people officer," Colleen McCreary, on how to offer constructive criticism and soften his persona.

ZYNGA GIVES BACK

Being so closely connected to the company, Pincus was personally affected by Zynga's problems as well. He watched his company face lawsuits and criticism and almost sever ties with Facebook. He led his company through the worst of it, but he still felt that something was missing. Pincus had seen how much of a difference it made when he worked on his own public image, and he intended to do the same for Zynga. One way he did this was by founding Zynga's charitable arm, Zynga.org.

Pincus had already pioneered the concept of virtual goods and saw how much money Zynga made from them. It seemed only right that the earning power of virtual goods be used to impart positive change in the world. With that thought in mind, he launched Zynga .org in October 2009. The philanthropic organization began as a platform within Zynga's games that allowed players to make contributions to charitable causes. Players had the option to purchase virtual goods to benefit a social cause instead of Zynga's bank account. Appropriately, Zynga called these special offerings "social goods." Zynga.org allocated the funds raised by these goods to various charities.

Pincus gives a talk at a Zynga event in San Francisco in 2011. Zynga has taken steps to give back to the world community through charitable endeavors.

Zynga's first social goods included "sweet seeds" for growing sweet potatoes that *FarmVille* players could purchase to benefit Haitian charities. As an added bonus for players, Zynga guaranteed that the crops would not wither (die). Later offerings included seeds for white corn and sugar beets. The social goods improved players' farms and helped them feel that they were playing for a cause beyond their own enjoyment. It was a smart and very successful move on Zynga's part.

By October 20, 2009, Zynga reported that players had raised $427,000 for Haitian charities through the purchase of social goods. Pincus was pleased. He said in a press statement, "The sheer scope and reach of social gaming to affect people's lives in a positive way wasn't even a reality a few years ago. With 'social goods,' we are enabling players to unlock their power to change the world and impact the lives of children."

Zynga.org launched at the right time. In the months after its launch, the world experienced many tragic events that affected the lives of millions of people. Zynga.org was in place to help. In response to Haiti's devastating earthquake in 2010, Zynga.org helped players raise $1.5 million in five days. One year later, Japan experienced an earthquake that displaced millions. Zynga.org announced that 100 percent of the proceeds from social goods would go to benefiting victims of that earthquake. A few weeks later, the company announced that pop superstar Lady Gaga had donated $750,000 to Zynga.org's relief fund. In all, the company raised more than $3 million for Japan's disaster relief.

Since its launch in late 2009, Zynga.org has raised more than $10 million for charities around the world. Millions of disadvantaged people have benefited from the sale of social goods. Mark Pincus had long known that social gaming could be powerful, but nobody could have predicted the way in which it would bring people together for a cause.

CHAPTER 6

Zynga Makes Moves

By 2010, Zynga had three years of success under its belt. During that time, both the company and its founder transitioned from inexperienced newbies to important figures in the industry. As Zynga grew, Mark Pincus matured as a CEO. Zynga's continued success began to silence his doubters. People respected his knowledge of social gaming. Bing Gordon told VentureBeat.com, "Mark has a spectacular insight when it comes to audience building, ease of use, and communication with friends." All of these qualities were foundational for Zynga's success. They would also serve him well as he prepared Zynga for the next phase of its growth—going public.

EXPANDING INTO FOREIGN MARKETS

Zynga's games were performing strongly in the United States, but Pincus knew that the company had to diversify in order to maintain its revenue stream and profitability.

This included exploring foreign markets and producing more hit games. If Zynga could accomplish these things, it would prove to the financial industry that it was ready to be a publicly traded company.

Pincus thought the best way to continue expanding was to break into foreign markets. He looked to Asia. The Asian countries had huge population numbers, and gaming was popular there. Unfortunately, Facebook wasn't the largest gaming platform in Asia, so he had to think outside the box. In May 2010, Zynga acquired XPD Media, a social gaming developer in China. Then, a few months later, Zynga announced that it had raised $150 million in investments from Softbank, a Japanese venture capital firm. The companies partnered to create Zynga Japan. Zynga's presence in Asia helped grow its user counts, and it provided the company with insight into the growing mobile gaming movement. This would later prove to be invaluable to Zynga's diversification.

YET ANOTHER HIT GAME

In the meantime, Zynga still had millions of players playing its games on Facebook. Numbers were strong, but they were stagnant. Expanding to foreign markets helped the company's growth, but it needed another hit like *FarmVille* to prove that it wasn't simply a one-hit wonder.

Pincus started putting pressure on his team to come up with the next hit. He put Mark Skaggs in charge of

CityVille launched in 2010 and quickly surpassed *FarmVille* as one of the most popular social games ever. *CityVille* helped earn the company a multibillion-dollar valuation before its IPO.

the project. By now, the Zynga team had its game launches down to a science. In 2010, Zynga launched *CityVille*, a game that put players in charge of their own cities. *CityVille* was a major hit. It launched in multiple languages to all of Zynga's markets, and it grew quickly from day one.

AppData reported that *CityVille* broke all previous social gaming records by amassing twenty-six million players in its first twelve days. As time went on, the game increased Zynga's monthly user counts to almost three hundred million. The game wasn't highly original (it used the same operating principles as *FarmVille*), but it proved that Zynga's formula worked. Zynga's ability to repeatedly turn out simple, social, and compelling games made people take notice. By the beginning of 2011, analysts gave the company a $5 billion valuation. The number made Zynga the highest-valued social gaming company ever.

GEARING UP TO GO PUBLIC

Pincus viewed these successes as proof that his company was ready to go public. In early 2011, he worked to get Zynga ready for its initial public offering (IPO). In February, he and his executive team began meeting with investors to raise more capital. Unlike the capital that Pincus raised in 2007, which helped cover operating expenses, this capital was intended to increase Zynga's worth. The higher the company's valuation, the higher its stock price would be at the initial public offering. This would benefit Pincus and other stockholders.

Aside from making itself more valuable, Zynga also sought to raise money for another reason—to help with acquisitions. According to an article in the *Wall Street Journal*, Zynga averaged about one acquisition a month during the year 2010–2011. The company did this for a few reasons. For one, it allowed Zynga to buy games that were already popular and generating revenue. For another, Zynga would be able to worry less about the next hot game coming from a competitor.

Zynga's increasing share of the social gaming market, as well as its increasing worth, eventually led to a valuation of $13 billion. Larry Albukerk, the managing director of investment firm EB Exchange Funds, told the *Wall Street Journal* that Zynga was one of the hottest Internet companies around, second only to Facebook. When Zynga's private valuations reached the multi-billion-dollar range, people suspected that it

What Is an IPO?

Many companies, especially start-ups like Zynga, begin as privately owned entities. Private companies get money from angel investors and venture capital firms that believe the companies will be successful. They invest with the hope that they will make more money back than they originally invested.

One measure of a company's success is when it grows to the degree that it can "go public." Going public means that anybody can invest in the company by purchasing its stock on a stock exchange. People purchase the company's stock in the form of shares. The more shares that a company sells, the more money the company brings in.

When a company sells its stock for the first time, it is called an initial public offering, or IPO. The original owners and investors finally have a chance to sell their shares to the public, allowing them to make back not only the money they originally invested but also more.

was preparing to go public. Pincus had known this for months, but it was only starting to become apparent to everyone else.

Zynga insiders and investors were excited about the company's public debut. However, many analysts felt that the company was overvalued. Others felt that there were too many risks associated with a relatively new Internet company. This was, perhaps, to be expected given the performance of many other technology companies' public debuts. For example, the popular daily deal Web site Groupon had been given a high valuation before going public. People later found out that the company's actual earnings did not warrant such a high valuation and stock price. People felt that this could be the case with Zynga— nobody truly knew the company's numbers except for Pincus and a handful of high-ranking executives.

Another major risk factor for Zynga was its dependence on Facebook. Any of the social network's successes or failures would directly affect Zynga. Zynga itself even identified this as a risk factor in its IPO filing, but the company was not worried. It had plans in the works to diversify away from Facebook, something it would announce in the coming months.

The analysts' doubts did not crush Zynga's excitement. The company's investors and personnel stood to make a lot of money from Zynga's public debut, especially Mark Pincus. As the company's largest shareholder, he was only a few short months away from becoming a billionaire.

A LETTER TO THE PUBLIC

Zynga filed an S-1 form with the U.S. Securities and Exchange Commission on July 1, 2011. The filing revealed some key financial numbers that people had wondered about for years. According to the filing, Zynga was on track to earn more than $1 billion in 2011. In the first quarter of 2011, the company brought in $235 million in revenue from the sale of virtual goods alone. Further, the public learned some interesting facts, such as Pincus's salary ($300,000 in 2011) and that he owned 16 percent of the company. The IPO filing helped paint a clearer picture of Zynga's strength. Further, it illuminated just how huge social gaming had become.

While most of the filing's focus was on the financial aspects of the company, Pincus shared something else with the public, too—the company's core values. In a letter to potential shareholders, he stated what Zynga was all about and reiterated his confidence in his company. According to Pincus's letter, Zynga's operating philosophies included the following:

- Games should be accessible to everyone, anywhere, anytime.
- Games should be social.

- Games should be free.
- Games should be data-driven.
- Games should do good.

Back in 2007, Pincus had launched Zynga with these beliefs in mind. The company had operated under these principles since its founding; the IPO filing was simply a way of declaring it to the public. By announcing these principles as its core values, Zynga would now be held accountable to shareholders and the general public to practice what it preached.

Pincus concluded this portion of the IPO filing with a major display of confidence: he put Zynga in the same category as top Internet companies such as Google, Facebook, and Amazon. In his letter to investors, Pincus wrote, "My kids decided a few months ago that peek-a-boo was their favorite game. While it's unlikely we can improve upon this classic, I look forward to playing Zynga games with them very soon. When they enter high school, there's no doubt that they'll search on Google, they'll share with their friends on Facebook, and they'll probably do a lot of shopping on Amazon. And I'm planning for Zynga to be there when they want to play."

The confidence that Pincus communicated in the IPO filing was noteworthy, as it told the public that Zynga—and Pincus—planned to be around for the long haul. Zynga, according to Pincus, was here to stay. With that, the company prepared itself for a huge milestone event—going public.

PUBLIC, AT LAST

Zynga went public on December 16, 2011. Its initial public offering was at $10 a share. This share price meant that Zynga was valued at $7 billion, or half of what was expected. Its stock price fluctuated throughout the day, and by the time the markets closed, it had settled at $9.50 a share.

Although it confirmed the company's worth to be $7 billion, news outlets such as *Forbes* and the *Wall Street Journal* declared that the IPO was "tepid" and "overhyped." These criticisms stemmed from the stock's performance: after debuting at $10, the stock price dropped 5 percent on its first day. After the IPO, shares continued to trade below the offering price. A number of factors caused investors to be hesitant about purchasing Zynga stock. Many people felt that Zynga's dependence on Facebook would be a problem down the road. Others thought that Zynga was just another trendy tech company that wouldn't last.

Regardless of the criticism, its IPO benefited its team immensely. With 16 percent ownership of the company, Pincus saw his net worth grow to $1.1 billion overnight. The company's original investors made out well, too. Kleiner Perkins, Union Square Ventures,

In preparation for its IPO, Zynga's logo was displayed on NASDAQ's electronic billboard for all of New York City to see. The company went public on December 16, 2011.

Foundry Venture Capital, Avalon Ventures, and investors like Reid Hoffman made millions from the stocks they held. They were pleased with their earnings and hoped that in the coming months, Zynga would trade around or above its offering price.

After the IPO, Pincus fielded many questions about Zynga's performance and what it meant for the social gaming giant. When the *Wall Street Journal* asked him about Zynga's "disappointing" IPO, he said, "I don't blame anybody because from our standpoint, we think it was successful. It was many times larger than the other tech IPOs that had just happened recently. We think we're now well positioned to move forward in the future."

With the IPO complete, Pincus prepared to take Zynga into new territory in 2012.

CHAPTER 7

Thinking Outside the Computer Screen

Before and after its IPO, Zynga had to show its stockholders that it had staying power. It had many risk factors leading up to its IPO, and one of the biggest was its dependence on Facebook. Mark Pincus knew that Zynga had to diversify in order to maintain its success. He knew that he could silence doubters if he showed the world that Zynga could evolve with the changing social gaming market.

THE WORLD GOES MOBILE

One of the most prominent changes in the tech world was the public's shift toward mobile Internet use. Smartphones debuted in the mid-'00s, but their popularity really took off around 2010. People began using their phones for everything, from making phone calls and browsing the Internet to using a variety of mobile

At a 2012 event, Pincus unveils the company's plans to develop games for several Web sites and mobile devices.

apps. Around the time Zynga went public, people were using their mobile phones just as much, if not more, than their regular computers. This presented a problem for Zynga, since all of its games were browser-based. It had no choice but to break into the mobile market.

Zynga held a press conference at its headquarters in San Francisco in October 2011. Just a few months before its IPO, Zynga announced that it would release ten mobile and social games on a variety of platforms. Not all of the games were ready to launch, but the company outlined its plans for diversification. The press conference revealed that Zynga had some games for mobile devices that were ready to go. The company also announced Project Z, its version of a social network. It would allow players to play Zynga's games on mobile platforms as well as computers. What's more, Zynga announced that *Mafia Wars 2* was available for play on Google+, a completely new platform for its games, and the continued expansion of its own FarmVille.com Web site. Zynga truly was diversifying, and the industry took note.

Pincus led the press conference with the same confidence that he demonstrated in Zynga's IPO filing. He spoke in front of a large audience of investors, analysts, press, and employees. It was a chance for him to brag about his employees' hard work in taking Zynga to the next level, as well as his own beliefs about Zynga's future. Because

Pincus was one of the founding fathers of social gaming, those in attendance took his opinion seriously. He closed the press conference by saying that Zynga was not only changing with the market, but it was also building its own platform to make games accessible to everyone. Closing the press conference, Pincus stated that Zynga was headed into the future with one goal in mind: "Everything behind what we are building is this mission to build a platform for play."

DRAW SOMETHING

In order to keep growing, Zynga kept acquiring smaller game companies and their popular games. In early 2012, independent game developer OMGPop launched *Draw Something*. The game was simple—users chose a word from a list and illustrated it for their friends to guess. *Draw Something* exploded in popularity, with thirty-five million downloads in its first month. What's more, the number of drawings generated on *Draw Something* exceeded one billion in that same time frame. The game's success caught Zynga's attention. Pincus knew he had to have it as part of the Zynga family. In March 2012, Zynga acquired OMGPop for $180 million.

Pincus placed a lot of hope on this acquisition and its ability to give Zynga a stronger foothold in the mobile market. However, a few weeks after the purchase,

An employee of OMGPop, the company that created *Draw Something*, uses his mobile device and tablet to draw a picture for his friend to guess. Zynga acquired OMGPop in early 2012.

the game's popularity collapsed. Zynga purchased the company at its peak of fifteen million users a day. But two weeks later, the game averaged only ten million users. Investors were unhappy with the game's performance, and it showed. Zynga's stock price fell, and the company was left wondering where it had gone wrong.

Afterward, the acquisition seemed like a hasty, unwise move. The company did not have an explanation beyond the fact that *Draw Something* was just a passing fad. Pincus took the failure in stride, and as recently as July 2012, he was telling inquiring minds that Zynga had big plans for the game that were yet to be revealed.

Pincus's Personal Life

Mark Pincus is so closely tied to Zynga that it is sometimes easy to forget that he has a life outside of work. But when you're the CEO of a corporation, you have to have interests outside of work to keep you balanced. Pincus tries to find balance by spending time with friends and family, as well as exploring hobbies that allow him to relax.

Pincus always loved gaming as a child, and the competitive drive that his family cultivated has followed him into his adult life. He enjoys playing sports, and he counts soccer and surfing as his two favorite outdoor activities. He plays soccer in a pickup league and has said that the lessons he's learned from playing on a soccer team have helped him run his company. He views surfing as a way to escape the pressures of work; when he's surfing, he can't have his Blackberry in tow. It helps him disconnect when he needs to. He likes to succeed at whatever he does, and he often pays for lessons to improve at one of his hobbies or learn a new one.

Pincus is also a family man. He married his wife, Ali, in 2010 and they have twin daughters, Carmen and Georgia. Family is important to Pincus both in and out of work, and he often brings his daughters to

Zynga's board meetings. Though they're still young, Pincus has said that he can't wait to play games with his children when they're older.

Pincus and his wife, Alison Gelb Pincus, attend a conference in Idaho in 2012. The couple married in 2010, and they have two children, twin daughters.

FACEBOOK GOES PUBLIC

Zynga had a lot to contend with in the months following its IPO. The acquisition of OMGPop and *Draw Something* did not go as hoped, but the company also experienced successes, including rolling out its mobile platform and diversifying its offerings.

Most of the news surrounding Zynga has been related to its performance in the stock market. While it debuted at a strong $10 per share, it has traded under that price since its first day. In July 2012, Zynga's stock price fell significantly. One reason was that the company reported much lower than expected earnings for the second quarter of the year. The company was also affected by one of the biggest events in the Internet industry—Facebook's IPO.

Facebook is one of the biggest Internet companies in history. Having been so successful over the years, many people anticipated that it would eventually go public. Finally, in 2012, Mark Zuckerberg decided to take the company public in what was one of the most highly anticipated IPOs ever. While the public was concentrating mainly on Facebook's stock, knowledgeable people understood that the debut would have a significant effect on Zynga. A successful IPO for Facebook would reflect positively on Zynga because of how closely the two companies work together. In fact, Zynga represents 10 percent of Facebook's revenue, so for either company to be successful, the other must be as well.

Facebook went public on May 18, 2012, and debuted at $42 a share. While it had a strong opening, the stock closed at $38 a share, and the price continued to decline after that day. Facebook's IPO was later called one of the most disappointing IPOs of all time.

Unfortunately, Zynga had to bear the burden of Facebook's unsuccessful IPO as well. Zynga's stock had been falling for months, and with investors' shaky confidence in Facebook, its biggest partner, Zynga's stock fell even more after Facebook's IPO. In July 2012, its stock had fallen a full 40 percent, to around $3 a share. The rumor mill started churning regarding Zynga's future, with some people even speculating that another company might acquire it.

THE FUTURE OF ZYNGA

Zynga's story has been a dramatic roller coaster ride. In just five years, what began as a tiny start-up with a team of eight people became a billion-dollar company with more than three thousand employees. Mark Pincus led Zynga every step of the way, facing equal amounts of criticism and praise. Zynga's many ups and downs have kept analysts on the edge of their seats, eager to see where the company is headed next.

A true pioneer, Pincus launched a wildly successful company in an industry that barely existed before Zynga. Today, Zynga's games are such a hallmark of our Internet culture that it's hard to imagine what life would be like without them. Without Pincus and Zynga, we might have never known what it's like to grow our own virtual corn or run our own virtual cities.

Through the company's highest highs and lowest lows, Pincus has looked to the future. By always thinking about Zynga's next step, he has helped the company diversify and stay relevant in an ever-changing industry. Whatever path Zynga takes as it heads into the future, it is a sure bet that Pincus will be there, pioneering the next big thing in social gaming.

Fact Sheet on

MARK PINCUS

Full Name: Mark Jonathan Pincus

Date of Birth: February 13, 1966

Birthplace: Chicago, Illinois

Parents: Theodore (Ted) and Sherri Pincus

Siblings: Four sisters: Anne, Laura, Jennifer, and Susan

Education: Bachelor's degree from the University of Pennsylvania; MBA from Harvard Business School

First Job: Financial analyst for Lazard Frères & Co.

Number of Companies Started: 4

Current Positions: CEO of Zynga, Inc.

Annual Salary at Zynga: About $300,000

Angel Investor for: Facebook, Twitter, and Napster

Current Residence: San Francisco, California

Marital Status: Married to Alison Gelb Pincus

Children: Twin daughters, Carmen and Georgia

Important Friends: Reid Hoffman and Mark Zuckerberg

Pets: Lola, an American bulldog

Hobbies: Soccer, surfing, and gaming

Quote from Mark Pincus:

"What's exciting in the five years since we started is that we've helped put play back in people's day… It is now a regular activity that everyday people do every day. And that's cool and exciting."

—*San Francisco Chronicle*, June 2012

Fact Sheet on

ZYNGA, INC.

Year Founded: 2007

Slogan: "Connecting the world through games."

Founder: Mark Pincus

Current CEO: Mark Pincus

Board of Directors: Mark Pincus, John Schappert, Bing Gorgon, Reid Hoffman, Jeffrey Katzenberg, Stanley J. Meresman, Sunil Paul, Ellen F. Siminoff, and Owen Van Natta

Headquarters: San Francisco, California

Number of Employees: About 3,000

Date Company Became Public: December 16, 2011

IPO Valuation: $7 billion

Stock Symbol: ZNGA

Annual Revenue: $1.16 billion in 2011

Number of Games: 48

Notable Games: *FarmVille, CityVille, Mafia Wars, Draw Something*

Number of Monthly Active Users: About 240 million (as of September 2012)

Number of Daily Active Users: About 60 million (as of September 2012)

Games Available In: 18 languages

Number of Studios/Subsidiaries: 19

Important Partnerships: Facebook

Philanthropic Organization: Zynga.org

Timeline

1966 Mark Jonathan Pincus is born on February 13 in Chicago, Illinois.

1984 Pincus graduates from high school and enters the University of Pennsylvania to study economics.

1992 Pincus interns at Bain & Company.

1993 Pincus graduates from Harvard Business School with his MBA.

1995 Pincus launches his first start-up, Freeloader, Inc.; Individual Co. acquires it seven months later for $38 million.

1997 Pincus launches Support.com, his second start-up.

2002 Pincus leaves Support.com.

2003 Pincus launches his third start-up and first social networking company, Tribe.net; Pincus and Reid Hoffman buy a social media patent for $700,000.

2006 Pincus leaves Tribe Networks and focuses on his next venture.

2007 Pincus proposes to his girlfriend, Alison Gelb, and she accepts; Presidio Media launches in April; in July, Pincus changes the company's name to Zynga; Zynga's first game, *Texas Hold 'Em Poker*, launches on Facebook.

2008 Psycho Monkey LLC files a lawsuit against Zynga, accusing Zynga of copying its *Mob Wars* game; Pincus meets Bing Gordon; Mark Skaggs joins Zynga as lead game developer.

2009 Zynga launches *FarmVille*, which becomes the most popular game on Facebook for eighteen months; Pincus is named CEO of the Year at the Crunchies Awards in San Francisco.

2010 Facebook and Zynga nearly part ways over a disagreement regarding in-game currency; the companies come to an agreement and announce a five-year partnership; Pincus's twin daughters, Carmen and Georgia, are born; *CityVille* surpasses *FarmVille* as Zynga's most popular game; Pincus receives the Crunchies Founder of the Year award.

2011 Zynga files an S-1 form with the U.S. Securities and Exchange Commission and aims to raise $1 billion dollars before its IPO; Zynga announces that it is developing mobile games, as well as Project Z, its own gaming platform; Zynga goes public on December 16, making Pincus a billionaire; the company's stock debuts at $10 per share; Zynga reports an annual revenue of $1.16 billion.

2012 Zynga acquires OMGPop and *Draw Something*; in July, Zynga's stock drops to about $3 a share after the company reports lower than expected quarterly earnings; *Forbes* magazine estimates that Pincus's net worth has decreased to about $700 million.

Glossary

acquisition The purchase of one company by another through the purchase of its assets or the purchase of its shares.

angel investor A wealthy individual who provides capital to a start-up in exchange for part ownership.

antithetical Directly opposite or opposed; mutually incompatible.

application ("app") A computer program or piece of software designed to perform a specific task.

browser-based software A software application that can only be used inside of an Internet browser.

capital Money or other resources used to produce additional wealth.

chief executive officer (CEO) The top executive at a company, responsible for overseeing operations and making the company's biggest decisions.

demographic A section of the population that shares particular qualities, such as age, gender, or income.

diversify To enlarge or vary the range of products or the field of operation of a company.

entrepreneur A person who organizes and manages a new business and takes on the risks associated with it.

in-game currency Virtual money that is used to purchase goods in an online game or virtual world. It is usually purchased with real-world money.

initial public offering (IPO) The act of taking a privately owned company public by offering stock for sale to the public for the first time.

juggernaut A huge, powerful force or institution.

mobile game A video game that can be played on a smartphone, tablet, or other portable device.

net worth A measure of a person's total financial worth, calculated by finding the value of all of his or her assets, minus any amounts owed to others.

pioneer To originate or take part in the development of something.

profitability A measure of business success, calculated by comparing a business's profit to its expenses.

quintessence The perfect example of something.

share An equal, usually small, part of a company's stock.

social gaming Playing games as a way to interact with other people, usually on a social networking platform.

social media Web and mobile technologies that allow users to connect with each other and share user-generated content.

social network A dedicated Web site or application that enables users to create a profile and form communities; users can then communicate with each other by posting information, comments, messages, and images.

start-up A new company that exists to find a successful and repeatable business model within a certain industry.

venture capital Money used for investment in new enterprises that involve high risk but offer the possibility of large profits.

virtual goods Non-physical objects that can be purchased for use in an online game or virtual world.

For More Information

Canadian Gaming Association (CGA)

131 Bloor Street West, Suite 503

Toronto, ON M5S 1P7

Canada

(416) 304-7800

Web site: http://www.canadiangaming.ca

This nonprofit organization is a source of accurate data about the gaming industry in Canada and is the national voice for the industry.

Entertainment Software Association (ESA)

575 7th Street NW, Suite 300

Washington, DC 20004

(202) 223-2400

Web site: http://www.theesa.com

The ESA serves the business and public affairs needs of companies that publish computer and video games for game consoles, personal computers, and the Internet.

Facebook, Inc.

1601 Willow Road

Menlo Park, CA 94025

(650) 543-4800

Web site: http://newsroom.fb.com

Facebook is the world's largest social networking site.
People use it to stay connected with friends and family,
discover what's going on in the world, and play games,
including those from Zynga.

International Game Developers Association (IGDA)

19 Mantua Road

Mount Royal, NJ 08061

(856) 423-2990

Web site: http://www.igda.org

The International Game Developers Association is the
largest nonprofit membership organization that serves
people who create video games.

On-Line Gamers Anonymous

P.O. Box 67

Osceola, WI 54020

(612) 245-1115

Web site: http://www.olganon.org

On-Line Gamers Anonymous is a support group that aims
to assist people with gaming addictions and problems
caused by excessive game playing.

TechCrunch

410 Townsend Street

San Francisco, CA 94107

Web site: http://www.techcrunch.com

Through its network of Web sites, TechCrunch is
dedicated to sharing the latest in technology-
related news. It reviews start-ups, digital products,
gadgets, and more.

Zynga, Inc.

699 8th Street

San Francisco, CA 94103

(855) 449-9642

Web site: http://www.zynga.com

Zynga is a developer and provider of popular social
games like *FarmVille*, *CityVille*, and *Mafia Wars*.
Its games are available on many global platforms,
including Facebook, Zynga.com, Google+, Tencent,
Apple iOS, and Google Android. Through Zynga.
org, Zynga players have raised more than $10
million for social causes.

Zynga Toronto, Inc.

218 Adelaide Street West, Suite 400

Toronto, ON MH5 1W7

Canada

(416) 479-0334

Web site: http://www.zynga.com

Zynga's Canadian subsidiary develops mobile applications for a variety of platforms. Before its
acquisition by Zynga in July 2011, it was known as
Five Mobile, Inc.

WEB SITES

Due to the changing nature of Internet links, Rosen
Publishing has developed an online list of Web sites
related to the subject of this book. This site is updated
regularly. Please use this link to access the list:

http://www.rosenlinks.com/IBIO/Zynga

For Further Reading

Brathwaite, Brenda, and Ian Schreiber. *Breaking into the Game Industry: Advice for a Successful Career from Those Who Have Done It.* Boston, MA: Course Technology/Cengage Learning, 2012.

Computer and Video Game Design (Ferguson's Careers in Focus). 2nd ed. New York, NY: Ferguson, 2009.

Crooks, Clayton E. *iPhone Game Development for Teens.* Boston, MA: Course Technology/Cengage Learning, 2013.

Fields, Tim, and Brandon Cotton. *Social Game Design: Monetization Methods and Mechanics.* Waltham, MA: Morgan Kaufman, 2012.

Funk, Joe, John Gaudiosi, and Dean Takahashi. *Hot Jobs in Video Games: Cool Careers in Interactive Entertainment.* New York, NY: Scholastic, 2010.

Mancusi, Marianne. *Gamer Girl.* New York, NY: Dutton Children's Books, 2008.

Marcovitz, Hal. *Online Gaming and Entertainment* (Issues in the Digital Age). San Diego, CA: ReferencePoint Press, 2012.

Miles, Liz. *Games: From Dice to Gaming* (Timeline History). Chicago, IL: Heinemann-Raintree, 2011.

Morales, Angela, and Kyle Orland. *FarmVille for Dummies.* Hoboken, NJ: Wiley, 2011.

Obee, Jennifer. *Social Networking: The Ultimate Teen Guide* (It Happened to Me). Lanham, MA: Scarecrow Press, 2012.

Orland, Kyle, and Michelle Oxman. *CityVille for Dummies.* Hoboken, NJ: Wiley, 2011.

Rankin, Kenrya. *Start It Up: The Complete Teen Business Guide to Turning Your Passions into Pay.* San Francisco, CA: Zest Books, 2011.

Ray, Michael. *Gaming: From Atari to Xbox* (Computing and Connecting in the 21st Century). New York, NY: Britannica Educational Publishing, 2011.

Rogers, Scott. *Level Up! The Guide to Great Video Game Design.* Hoboken, NJ: Wiley, 2010.

Saylor, Michael. *The Mobile Wave: How Mobile Intelligence Will Change Everything.* New York, NY: Vanguard Press, 2012.

Swaine, Meg. *Career Building Through Interactive Online Games* (Digital Career Building). New York, NY: Rosen Publishing, 2008.

Takahashi, Dean. *Zynga: From Outcast to $9 Billion Social-Game Powerhouse.* Kindle ed. San Francisco, CA: VentureBeat, 2011.

Unger, Kimberly, and Jeannie Novak. *Mobile Game Development* (Game Development Essentials). Clifton Park, NY: Delmar/Cengage Learning, 2012.

Wilkinson, Colin. *Gaming: Playing Safe and Playing Smart* (Digital and Information Literacy). New York, NY: Rosen Central, 2012.

Wyman, Michael Thornton. *Making Great Games: An Insider's Guide to Designing and Developing the World's Greatest Video Games.* Burlington, MA: Focal Press, 2010.

Bibliography

Arrington, Michael. "Scamville: The Social Gaming Ecosystem of Hell." TechCrunch.com, October 31, 2009. Retrieved July 20, 2012 (http://techcrunch.com/2009/10/31/scamville-the-social-gaming-ecosystem-of-hell).

Arrington, Michael. "Zynga CEO Mark Pincus: 'I Did Every Horrible Thing in the Book Just to Get Revenues.'" TechCrunch.com, November 6, 2009. Retrieved September 11, 2012 (http://techcrunch.com/2009/11/06/zynga-scamville-mark-pinkus-faceboo).

Bryant, Adam. "Mark Pincus—Every Worker Should Be C.E.O. of Something." *New York Times*, January 30, 2010. Retrieved June 1, 2012 (http://www.nytimes.com/2010/01/31/business/31corner.html?pagewanted=all).

Grigoriadis, Vanessa. "Ol' Mark Pincus Had A Farm…" *Vanity Fair*, June 2011. Retrieved June 17, 2012 (http://www.vanityfair.com/business/features/2011/06/mark-pincus-farmville-201106).

Gross, Doug. "The Facebook Games That Millions Love (and Hate)." CNN.com, February 23, 2010. Retrieved June 17, 2012 (http://articles.cnn.com/2010-02-23/tech/facebook.games_1_mark-pincus-video-games-facebook?_s=PM:TECH).

Guy, Sandra. "Mark Pincus Creates an Empire with Games Designed for Facebook." *Chicago Sun-Times*, March 27,

2011. Retrieved June 19, 2012 (http://www.suntimes
.com/4534296-417/mark-pincus-creates-an-empire
-with-games-designed-for-facebook.html).

Hendrickson, Matt. "Why You Should Love the Most
Hated Man on Facebook." *Details*, May 2010.
Retrieved July 19, 2012 (http://www.details.com/style
-advice/tech-and-design/201005/mark-pincus-facebook
-mafia-wars-farmville-zynga?currentPage=1).

Hirschman, David. "So What Do You Do, Mark Pincus,
CEO of Zynga?" Mediabistro.com, September 16, 2009.
Retrieved June 1, 2012 (http://www.mediabistro.com/
articles/details.asp?aID=10636&).

Hof, Robert. "Zynga IPO Goes SplatVille. What Went
Wrong?" *Forbes*, December 16, 2011. Retrieved
July 26, 2012 (http://www.forbes.com/sites/
roberthof/2011/12/16/zynga-ipo-goes-splatville
-what-happened).

Kim, Ryan. "Tapping into Growing Market for Virtual
Goods." *San Francisco Chronicle*, November 2, 2009.
Retrieved July 25, 2012 (http://www.sfgate.com/
business/article/Tapping-into-growing-market-for
-virtual-goods-3282368.php).

LaVallee, Andrew. "App Watch: 11 Million Facebookers
Flock to *FarmVille*." WSJ.com, August 31, 2009.
Retrieved July 19, 2012 (http://blogs.wsj.com/
digits/2009/08/31/app-watch-facebooks
-11-million-farmers).

Naone, Erica. "Marketing Virtual Goods: Q&A with Zynga's Mark Pincus." *Technology Review*, October 15, 2010. Retrieved July 3, 2010 (http://www.technologyreview.com/news/421220/marketing-virtual-goods-qa-with-zyngas-mark).

Nuttall, Chris. "The Tech World's Willy Wonka." *Financial Times*, May 6, 2012. Retrieved July 3, 2012 (http://www.ft.com/intl/cms/s/0/f7ff2b72-942a-11e1-bb47-00144feab49a.html#axzz22JYBtpDE).

Raice, Shayndi. "Zynga CEO Mark Pincus Calls IPO a Success, Concedes Missteps." *Wall Street Journal*, January 17, 2012. Retrieved July 29, 2012 (http://online.wsj.com/article/SB10001424052970204409004577158744071030040.html?mod=WSJ_Tech_LEADTop).

Rose, Charlie. "Charlie Rose—Mark Pincus 12/28/09." YouTube.com, December 30, 2009. Retrieved July 25, 2012 (http://www.youtube.com/watch?v=Exi-n5hXZQY).

Rusli, Evelyn M. "Zynga's Tough Culture Risks a Talent Drain." *New York Times*, November 27, 2011. Retrieved July 29, 2012 (http://dealbook.nytimes.com/2011/11/27/zyngas-tough-culture-risks-a-talent-drain).

Startup@Berkeley. "Mark Pincus Talk at Startup@Berkeley." Vimeo.com, March 18, 2009. Retrieved June 5, 2012 (http://vimeo.com/3738428).

U.S. Securities and Exchange Commission. "Form S-1 Registration Statement—Zynga, Inc." July 1, 2011.

Retrieved July 31, 2012 (http://www.sec.gov/Archives/ edgar/data/1439404000119312511180285/ds1.htm).

Wingfield, Nick, Spencer E. Ante, and Anupreeta Das. "Zynga Valuation Rises to Over $7 Billion." *Wall Street Journal*, February 14, 2011. Retrieved July 29, 2012 (http://online.wsj.com/article_email/SB1000142405 27487035155045761426934084 73796-lMyQjAxMT AxMDEwMzExNDMyWj.html).

Wollan, Malia. "Sunday Routine—Filling a Day with Everything Nice." *New York Times*, May 8, 2010. Retrieved July 14, 2012 (http://www.nytimes .com/2010/05/09/us/09sfroutines.html?_r=1).

WSJ Digital Network. "Mark Pincus on Zynga and Facebook—D10 Conference." YouTube.com, May 30, 2012. Retrieved July 26, 2012 (http://www.youtube.com/ watch?v=Avo7AcfX46s&feature=related).

Index

ABOUT THE AUTHOR

Sarah Machajewski is an author and journalist who has written more than fifty books on subjects ranging from science to history. She witnessed the rise of social media from her dorm room at college, having spent many hours logged into Facebook and other Internet forums. She considers social networking to be an integral part of her life and enjoyed researching Zynga and its influence on the Internet community. Machajewski graduated from the University of Pittsburgh in 2010 and currently lives in Buffalo, New York, with her family.

PHOTO CREDITS

Cover, pp. 3, 34, 37, 40, 46–47, 54–55, 68–69, 74–75, 78–79, 97 Bloomberg/Getty Images; pp. 6–7 ZUMA Press/Newscom; p. 12 Jim Wilson/The New York Times/Redux; pp. 14–15, 25 (top and bottom), 52–53, 60–61, 81, 86–87, 94 © AP Images; pp. 18–19 Peter DaSilva/The New York Times/Redux; pp. 28–29 Brendan O'Sullivan/Photolibrary/GettyImages; p. 30 © Susan Ragan/The New York Times/Redux; p. 42 Business Wire/Getty Images; pp. 58–59 Zynga/AP Images; pp. 64–65 Jay Janner/MCT/Landov; pp. 100–101 Jennifer S. Altman/The New York Times/Redux; p. 103 Kevork Djansezian/Getty Images; pp. 20, 21, 30, 31, 42, 43, 72, 73, 89, 102, 103 kentoh/Shutterstock.com; cover and remaining interior background image dpaint/Shutterstock.com.

Designer: Brian Garvey; Editor: Andrea Sclarow Paskoff; Photo Researcher: Karen Huang